Getting Started With PhoneGap 4

Matthew Ray

Edited by Britney Earwood

ISBN-13: 978-1500187705

ISBN-10: 1500187704

dedication

To my daughter, Reese, who continues to enforce the idea that the world is a wondrous place where things that seem impossible are really just problems to be slept on.

And to Ashley for living through my nerd-dom everyday.

contents

acknowledgments

This book would not be possible were it not for the amazing effort of the PhoneGap team and the contributors to the Apache Cordova project. Without their continuous improvement of the framework and toolsets, many great ideas would remain in stasis, never to cross over into existence.

I would also like to acknowledge the work of the user community who post and answer questions constantly in online forums and pave the way for a deeper understanding of the systems at play.

Thanks to my parents for the Commodore 64 (and BASIC manual I digested at 10), the Visual Basic 4 for Christmas (at age 15), and the incredible support and encouragement (all ages). My little sister for becoming a geek, so I had someone to talk about these things with.

Thank you to my friends and coworkers at eImagine Technology Group (http://thinketg.com) who took a chance on me when I told them I could perform a sort of "magic act" by turning HTML, CSS, and JavaScript into mobile apps for the masses.

Lastly, this book would not be what it is without my editor, Britney Earwood, constantly cleaning up my mess. Seriously.

introduction

1

PhoneGap is a set of command-line tools and libraries that allow developers–specifically, web developers–to write real, installable app-store-listed mobile apps using common web technologies such as HTML, CSS, and JavaScript. It exists to provide a neutral ground from which mobile apps can be written while being platform agnostic. This is due to PhoneGap providing mechanisms for building a single source tree into all of the popular mobile device platform formats: iOS, Android, and Windows Phone.

The framework functions by generating scaffolding—a series of folders and files that make up a template by which to work. Folders and default files exist within the scaffolding for overarching styles (CSS), front-facing user interface (HTML), as well as the code to provide interactivity and functionality (JavaScript). During the generation process, PhoneGap also adds some hidden framework folders and files to the project that enable the JavaScript calls to take advantage of native hardware features once deployed onto a device.

The way PhoneGap accomplishes its magic lies in the way it generates the application shell itself. When a developer builds to a given mobile environment, PhoneGap runs a series of scripts to instantiate a copy of a built-in app shell template for the corresponding platform and merge it with the updated web files. This template-generated app is very similar for each platform in that it essentially contains a single-view app with a full-screen web browser embedded in it and some native instruction to parse a configuration file for developer-selected options and instructions and then load the "index.html" file from the merged web content.

For the end user, the experience is identical to installing and launching any other app they have used on their device. For you, the developer, the experience is significantly different than native application development in that you are tapping into a rich, evolved, and highly-supported history of web application development and a larger community of support.

Writing web apps to cater to mobile isn't something new. In fact, you can trace the roots of PhoneGap back to a critical juncture in mobile computing history and, in doing so, understand how the need arose for such a thing.

On June 29, 2007, the very first version of the iPhone became available for purchase. That initial entry by Apple into the smartphone market is regarded as perhaps the most disruptive event in mobile phone and mobile computing history. With its tremendous success came a bold statement from Apple: Web applications could provide rich user experiences without requiring developers to dive into platform-specific code.

It is certainly worth explaining that, when asked about 3rd party app support, Apple's initial answer was there was no need for an app store or 3rd party apps as the iOS operating system supported use of Web 2.0 web apps. Developers at the time were aghast they would not be able to immediately provide the same level of polish that was clearly visible with the Apple-produced native applications such as Mail, Safari, and Calendar.

Apple quickly reversed course. On October 27 of that same year, an open letter from Steve Jobs announced an official software development kit (SDK) that would be made available the next year. By the middle of 2008, Apple released a new iteration of the iOS operating system and the official app store with it.

In my humble opinion, this brief period where it seemed that web apps might finally gain broader, more robust support from an industry heavyweight, only to be snuffed out less than a year later, should be recognized as a huge setback for the app development community. That might not seem congruent with the state of mobile app development by the numbers with Apple announcing in late 2013 the arrival of its millionth entry. While I certainly cannot argue that the development community has done quite well for itself in this short period of time, I do argue that it could have gone significantly smoother and been even more technologically disruptive than what we have experienced thus far.

As backwards as this may seem, I can't help but wonder where we would be if Apple had not given in to the development community that was crying out for an official SDK and an app store. In my imaginings, I see Apple holding strong to the idea that web apps could gain access to the same hardware components as the apps that Apple had distributed. In order to make that happen and make good on the promise of enabling web apps, Apple might have been pressured to strengthen the support for all things "web" by providing more timely access to the camera, microphone, geolocation, gyroscopic, and storage components—the foundational value of the HTML5 spec.

On the back of such expanded functionality, web apps—and the ability to install them as a static entity that doesn't require network accessibility—might have taken off and gained broader support by Apple's largest competitors, Google and Microsoft. At that point, the entire web ecosystem might have benefited from innovations in JavaScript processing, UI toolkit expansion, and hardware accessibility.

But that isn't what happened. Instead, support for much of the aforementioned hardware is still limited in native JavaScript implementations and is often accessible only through specific browsers on specific platforms. This necessitates some sort of substrate by which the features and benefits of native application development can be bound to the widespread world of web application development. This is precisely the space that PhoneGap exists in.

PhoneGap has grown substantially from its roots as a hacked-together toolset that allowed JavaScript access to the geolocation data on an iPhone into a mature toolset that is ready for primetime. Since its inception, Adobe has acquired Nitobi, the caretakers behind PhoneGap. At the same time as the Nitobi acquisition, the core of PhoneGap, named Cordova, was placed into the capable and incubating hands of the Apache Software Foundation. This has enabled a public and highly-visible open source continuation of the software framework that has already enabled thousands of applications to be conceived.

In the latest version, PhoneGap supports a wide array of hardware variations and capabilities, providing JavaScript API access to accelerometer data, video capture and playback, file storage and synchronization, and many more features. As new devices and peripherals such as Bluetooth-connected wearables come to market, developers are quick to take the public software development kits (SDKs) or application programming interfaces (APIs) and create PhoneGap-compatible plug-ins to provide easier access for the PhoneGap community.

It is a great time for newcomers to join the PhoneGap developer community or for veterans of prior releases to brush up on the latest capabilities in PhoneGap 4.x. New tools and capabilities are always being added along with the usual round of bug fixes.

Before jumping straight into the code, let's make sure you have the tools you need to successfully dive into developing with PhoneGap 4.

2 preparing your system

Before you begin the process of installing or updating your software to conform to the PhoneGap development requirements, it is important to understand the potential limitations that may be introduced simply by the hardware or operating system from which you work. For instance, you can install and build for the Google Android platform on nearly any type of system: Linux, Windows, or Mac. To build and distribute apps for the Apple iOS set of devices, however, the tools required to do so are intentionally built against the Mac OSX operating system and will not work in other environments (despite OSX being a cleverly orchestrated window manager for Unix itself). Similarly, Windows Phone app compiling and distribution is limited to tools based on the Windows operating system–specifically Windows 8 or higher—to reach the newer mobile devices.

The quick reference chart ahead (*2.1: Platform Reference*) can give you an easy reference to help you determine the platforms you can build for given your existing hardware or, perhaps, consider what combination will yield you the most ubiquitous approach. With that in mind, there is another option available, particularly to those running on Mac hardware, that can allow you to cover all of the options on one machine: virtualization.

Virtualization allows a user, a developer in this case, to run an operating system that is either configured specifically to run within a specific hardware environment or to run on hardware that it may not have originally been intended for. Servers may run multiple concurrent virtual machines (VMs) on a single hardware appliance, allowing sandboxed environments while further commoditizing hardware.

For developers, this is useful in utilizing the hardware-agnostic features on some virtualization systems to overcome the demands of publishing to platforms that may not always be readily available. PhoneGap developers also find that debugging can be a bit easier as virtual machines can be configured to share resources—hard drive space, specifically—with the host machine. This allows the single source tree to be shared amongst the various virtual machines.

For many years, I have worked from a MacBook and utilized software such as Parallels Desktop and VMware Fusion to allow me to run the Windows operating system within my Mac environment. And while other options are available, these two commercial products provide great support and don't require manipulation of configuration files and unsupported "hacks" to ensure continued compatibility and use. Their use further facilitates flexibility in being able to open Windows Phone builds within

Visual Studio and utilize the required Windows Phone SDK to produce the appropriate packages to upload to the Windows Phone App Store.

2.1: Platform Reference	
Mobile Platform	**Development OS**
Android	Windows, Mac OSX, Linux
iOS	Mac OSX
Windows Phone	Windows

The first component we will need to install, regardless of platform, is Node.js. According to the official Node.js web site, "Node.js is a platform built on Chrome's JavaScript runtime for easily building fast, scalable network applications. Node.js uses an event-driven, non-blocking I/O model that makes it lightweight and efficient, perfect for data-intensive real-time applications that run across distributed devices."

What that really means is Node.js provides a flexible platform that allows developers to create JavaScript-based applications that function as a server-side system completely independent of a browser, the traditional sandbox JavaScript is meant to run in. Much like PhoneGap itself, Node.js has an aim to take something that is rather ubiquitous (JavaScript programming) and make it available in areas where it was previously inaccessible or thought to be inefficient.

In recent times, there has been some concern and discussion around just how far the concept of extending JavaScript can or should be taken. For instance, security concerns have arisen as some have sought to utilize the platform for monetary transactions using module or packages that may not be secure themselves, thus potentially opening up vulnerabilities to end users.

That being said, our uses of Node.js are pretty straightforward: it serves as the platform whereby we can run the PhoneGap system locally, generating new PhoneGap applications or initiating builds that are then fed through the appropriate SDK toolchains. Since all of our interaction will be confined to our local machine, standard security practices (firewall, antivirus, etc.) will suffice to ensure the safety of our development machine.

To install Node.js, go to http://nodejs.org in your browser and follow the installation steps, including the download necessary to begin. We will walk through these steps briefly on the next few pages, but understand they may change in future releases. At the time of publication, these instructions are valid as of release 0.10.29.

2.2: Installing Node.js

1. Visit http://nodejs.org.

2. Click the INSTALL button as seen in the image to the right.

3. Save the file to your local drive.

4. Run the saved file (a PKG or EXE file).

5. You will be presented with a screen similar to the following:

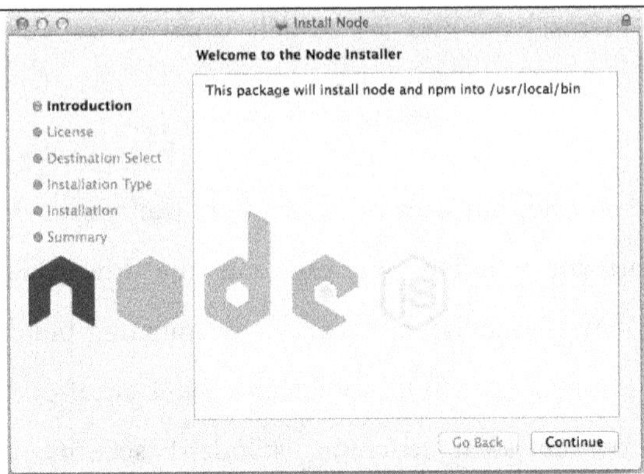

6. Click continue and read and agree to the licensing terms.

7. You may be asked to authorize the installation of system files in a dialog similar to the screen below. This is normal and required for Node.js to perform properly. Authenticate with your administrative credentials to continue and click the INSTALL SOFTWARE button.

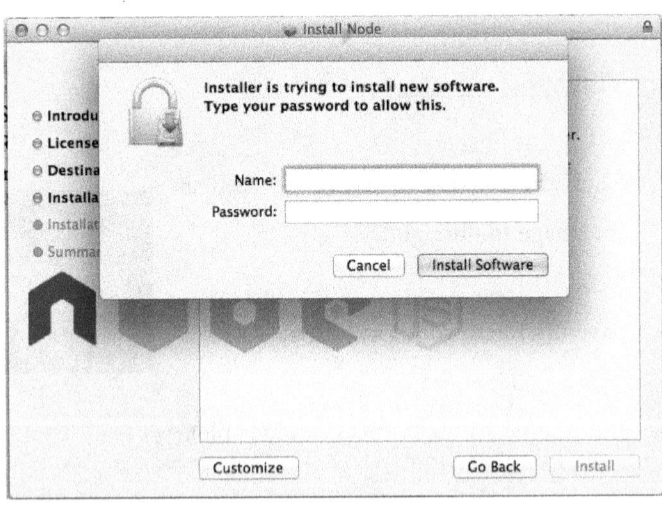

8. Once installation is complete, the installer will note the location of the executable Node.js system for reference, though you will not likely need this information.

With Node.js installed, we can test the installation and make sure all is working properly. The easiest way to do this is to open a command line prompt and execute the Node Package Manager (NPM) tool by simply entering:

```
npm -v
```

With this command we are requesting that NPM indicate what version it is. If you see a response indicating a version (mine currently reads "1.4.14"), then all is well. It is worth noting this utility is frequently used in developing for PhoneGap due to the frequent release of new versions.

With Node.js installed and tested, we can install the actual PhoneGap toolset. The installation process utilizes the Node.js platform installed in the prior step, invoking the NPM tool again. In doing so, this will also demonstrate the current method whereby new and updated versions of the PhoneGap toolset are installed on your machine.

On Windows, use the following command to install PhoneGap:

```
npm install –g phonegap
```

On a Mac or Linux system, use the following command to install PhoneGap:

```
sudo npm install –g phonegap
```

As PhoneGap is installing, you will notice that the Node Package Manager is retrieving the dependencies, libraries, and tools that are required for the correct operation of the PhoneGap package and tools as well as installing them where appropriate. This is displayed to you as a series of requests to web resources (http/https) and then progresses as it downloads the packages.

When PhoneGap is finished installing, you can test the validity of your instance by executing the following version request on the PhoneGap tool:

```
phonegap –v
```

Much like with the testing of the Node.js installation, the command above should return a version response. If, for some reason, it does not and you receive an indication that the command is unknown to your system, verify that the appropriate "-g" flag was added to the installation command. This switch is essential to signaling the Node Package Manager to create a global link to the PhoneGap system and prevents you having to explicitly state the path to the executable each time. Trust me, you are going to want that flag on there.

It is also worth noting that you can add @<version> where <version> is replaced with a specific release number to the end of the PhoneGap installation command in order to install that release. From time to time, there may be reason to do this as even the most diligent testing on the part of the PhoneGap team may not catch a bug that could affect your specific implementation or app, necessitating a rollback to a prior version where the bug does not exist. Here is an example that illustrates the installation of PhoneGap version 3.1 (an older build) on a Mac or Linux system:

```
sudo npm install –g phonegap@3.1.0-0.15.0
```

With the PhoneGap toolset now running correctly, you can consider the device-specific libraries and interfaces you may need. Again, some of this may be restricted based on the hardware and/or operating system you are running.

If you wish to build for Android devices, you must install a bundle of software including the Android SDK and platform tools. It is highly recommended that you also install an Integrated Development Environment (IDE) that directly supports the Android toolset. Doing so dramatically eases the process of creating signed packages and binary builds that you will need to deploy to devices beyond those you are debugging on.

Thankfully, the Android team has made available all of the software packages and components needed, bundled together into a single download. This can currently be found at:

http://developer.android.com/sdk/index.html

The downloadable bundle consists of a zip file that must be unpacked on your development machine. You can use your preferred or default "unzipping" application for this task, often by double-clicking or right-clicking the downloaded zip file and choosing the option to expand or unpack the contents.

Once unpacked, you will find an "eclipse" folder and an "sdk" folder. If you are not familiar with Eclipse or developing for the Android platform, it is recommended that you keep the two folders ("eclipse" and "sdk") together as a pair wherever you decide to keep them long-term. If, however, this isn't feasible or you are feeling adventurous and want to split them up, you may always modify the path to your SDKs in the Eclipse settings and preferences.

Eclipse is an Integrated Development Environment (IDE) meant to simplify common tasks and provide a visual tool for more easily managing development—particularly of Java-based targets such as Android applications (but it is certainly not limited to this). You can relocate these folders to permanent locations of your choosing, taking care to memorize or otherwise record the final locations you chose as you may need to reset the aforementioned SDK location.

You can run Eclipse anytime now by executing the Eclipse app found in the "eclipse" folder.

2.3: Android SDK Setup

You will likely need to install additional components from within Eclipse and, because these change frequently, those instructions will not be covered here. A good resource for this is the Android developer portal. As of this printing, those instructions are located at:

https://developer.android.com/sdk/installing/adding-packages.html

If you intend to develop for the iOS platform, catering to the millions of iPod, iPhone, and iPad devices in consumer hands, you will need to ensure that Apple's Xcode development system is installed and setup for use.

Apple has made it quite simple to get the Xcode system. You can find it by opening the App Store on your Mac and searching for "Xcode." While it is a free download, it can be quite large and take a while to get installed. I recommend using a high-speed internet connection and, if permitted, letting it download overnight.

Once installed, Xcode may ask if you wish to download optional components such as command-line tools and you will want to do so as they will come in handy later on in development. If, however, you are not asked this when you launch Xcode, you may download the optional components by going to Xcode Preferences and choosing the Downloads tab.

The last major platform that you may need to install is Visual Studio for targeting the Windows Phone operating system. To do this you must be on a Windows platform, either via native installation or running in a virtual machine on another platform as mentioned previously.

If you already have Visual Studio installed, as many developers who have access to the Windows platform do, you do not need to reinstall Visual Studio and can jump right to the installation of the Windows Phone SDK. Visual Studio does currently come in an "express" version (free) that you can use for purposes of performing app builds.

2.4: Visual Studio with Cordova

In the past year, a few Community Technology Preview (CTP) editions of Visual Studio have been released by Microsoft with the base Cordova toolset integrated into the Visual Studio environment. While an official public version has not been released yet, it is clear that Microsoft sees some value in more closely aligning their mobile strategy to be in line with the ideals of the Cordova team. So, if you are an existing developer comfortable with the Microsoft development environment and mechanics, it is quite likely that the next major version of Visual Studio will provide much of the mechanics discussed here in an integrated and contextual way, most likely through menu choices and is probably something to watch for.

To install Visual Studio, first download the installer from Microsoft by visiting the following location in your browser:

http://www.visualstudio.com/

Once there, look for the downloads section of the site and then the "Express" version download for your platform. Download the installer to a safe location on your desktop (or virtual machine) and execute the installer.

If, during the installation process, you have the opportunity to install the Windows Phone SDK, you should do so as this will eliminate an additional step post-installation.

2.5: Windows Phone SDK

Currently the Windows Phone SDK is shipped with the most recent versions of Visual Studio, so it is likely the SDK will be installed as part of this package.

While not strictly required for PhoneGap development, one of the last components you may want to install is a method of source control. If you are unfamiliar with source control or code versioning, take a look at the inset below.

2.6: What is Source Control?
I like to think of source control as a development analogue for the "save game" system in most modern video games. In a game, your character or progress is at risk of being lost: enemies might unexpectedly defeat you or the power might even go off, rendering your time playing into a wasted effort. Saving your game progress, however, reduces the impact of such events as you only have to restart from the point of the last save. Source control and code versioning systems attempt to do the same with developing code, since it can be perilous as well: a well-meaning code change can accidentally inject a bug that may not be caught for several iterations. Tracking down the state of things before the bug was introduced can be an arduous task unless you could simply "load a save point" and compare code back to when that bug was nonexistent. While solid source control implementation can assist in many more ways, this is the foundation of its use in professional development.

There are many source control mechanisms available for implementation including Git, Subversion, SVN, and Team Foundation Server (TFS) to name a few. The PhoneGap and Cordova communities have standardized on using Git both for app development and the method for injecting publicly-available plug-ins into an application.

It is highly recommended that you consider using Git and familiarizing yourself with the mechanics of it over another system. To find out more about the Git version management system, visit the following URL in you web browser:

http://git-scm.com/

Once everything is installed, it is a good idea to go back and run each of the applications (Xcode, Eclipse, Visual Studio, etc.) to ensure that no error messages or additional components need initialization. Potential hazards later in building for a particular platform can often be avoided simply by validating that an install was completed successfully at this stage.

If you happen to run into issues that do not have an obvious resolution, check the Troubleshooting section as it is likely something I have come across before. Failing that, the Troubleshooting section also provides a list of other resources I frequently engage with when attempting to resolve an issue.

3 generating your app

With your development environment set up and validated, we turn to the task of generating the scaffolding by which you will write a PhoneGap app. If the process of installation and configuration in the prior chapter left you feeling a bit shaken in your confidence, fear not. The syntax and options in generating a new app (or building an existing one) are very straightforward and few in number, which should allow you to memorize the command structure or, at a minimum, recall how to get quick help.

By now you should be comfortable opening a command prompt in your particular development machine's operating system. This is important as much of the execution of the build process is done through the command prompt.

The first step in creating an PhoneGap application is to generate the application folder and base template. You do this from the command line using the following command and format:

```
phonegap create <folder> <identifier> <title/name>
```

For demonstration purposes, we will create a new PhoneGap app—a game, actually. The purpose of the game, to be called "Clickin' Crazy," will be simple: get tap-happy on a button to raise a power meter to maximum.

To generate the application's default files, I run the following command, an expansion on the format prescribed above:

```
phonegap create clickincrazy com.clickincrazy.app ClickinCrazy
```

Once the command completes, PhoneGap will have taken the base templates for the version of PhoneGap currently installed and used them to generate a basic scaffold for your new app. The newly-created folder is named according to the first parameter ("clickincrazy," in this case) while the identifier and title parameters are added to a configuration file called config.xml.

3.1: What is the Identifier?
The identifier and title are not required, but with some forethought you will begin to use them when create your app. The identifier is used primarily when it comes time to place an app in the app store. The format of the identifier parameter is almost always reverse domain name notation, meaning that it is "backwards" from a traditional domain name. Even if you choose not to set one during the creation process you can always add one later by changing the default in the config.xml file.

Within the new folder exists several subfolders. The great news for you, as a developer, is that you can ignore most of these. More specifically, you should ignore most of these as modifying their contents can lead to issues in building and managing your new mobile app. The exception to this is the "www" folder which contains the default template files for creating your app and you will find yourself working within it extensively.

This is a great point to open up the "www" folder with the editor you plan to use for development. See the special section on page 24 for more information on choosing a good editor, if you have not yet settled on one.

From within the "www" folder, you can see a folder dedicated to your css, javascript, and images. In here, you will also find the index.html file that will serve as the starting point for your application and is the first HTML resource loaded when the app is opened.

Another folder is the "res" folder, a resources container that serves as a storage point for icons and splash screens for the platforms that PhoneGap is capable of producing builds for. Since the icons and splash screens are cropped to the specific sizes needed when the app is built or subsequently placed in the app store, you can use them as proportional guide for your customized versions.

Lastly, the "spec" folder contains the Jasmine unit testing framework and a few example entries to get you started. I would like to emphasize the importance of structured unit testing as you begin to develop public-facing mobile apps, as it can serve as a sort of "canary" to detect accidental breaks before they become public embarrassments.

With a better grasp of the file folders and structures at play, the best way to get a grasp for the mechanics is to simply open the index.html file in your browser. For this, I recommend Google's Chrome browser. The reason for recommending Chrome is simple: it contains a fairly new feature that allows viewing of web content within the constrained screen and pixel densities of select mobile devices. This handy feature is squarely aimed at developers for the purpose of validating the appearance and functionality of your web content. Additionally, Chrome continues to render web content in a manner consistent with the experience on an actual mobile device—Android, iOS, or otherwise.

After opening the index.html file, you may feel underwhelmed. It simply displays the PhoneGap logo with a "Connecting to Device" message utilizing an animated background. This is, of course, normal and is simply meant to demonstrate some of the events that PhoneGap can handle as an app starts up. You may wonder, however, "Why doesn't it connect?"

The reason it seems stuck in a continuous "connect" attempt is that the PhoneGap system relies on the build process to generate native chunks of code that create the substrate that the JavaScript can use to communicate with the target operating system. Because we have loaded this page in a plain desktop browser, that substrate doesn't exist and, therefore, the JavaScript that awaits connection with a mobile device's operating system isn't available.

To see the difference, perform the following steps:

1. Download the "PhoneGap Developer" app from your mobile device's app store (free from Adobe).
2. From the command prompt and within your app's project folder, run the command:

   phonegap serve
3. On your mobile device, launch the PhoneGap Developer app and set the URL to match the "listening on" information displayed as output of the "phonegap serve" command (an IP address and port assignment).
4. Click connect on the mobile device and, barring no firewall or configuration issues, the default app screen will load on the mobile device.

The difference you should immediately pick up on is the app is no longer stuck attempting to "connect." Instead, the app is able to establish the connection and display the appropriate message.

You can initiate this semi-native application link anytime using the same series of steps (excepting the need to download the PhoneGap Developer app each time). The framework is intelligent enough to reload the current view should a code change be implemented on the PC that would change the state of the mobile app currently being viewed. As an example, you could completely remove the UI components from the index.html page and, upon saving, see them disappear from your mobile device's view. More on this is covered later in the section on debugging.

With the app generated and demonstrated, it's time to build something worth showing off.

3.2: What to Look For in an Editor

Like many things, choosing the perfect editing application for you can be a matter of personal taste. However, there are some core features you should look for in an editor that will make the process of developing in HTML, CSS, and JavaScript a more fruitful use of your time.

Code Highlighting: This simple but important piece allows you to better visualize tiny mistakes in the code. For instance, you might be tipped off to an unterminated quotation mark by a large block of text appearing to be the same color.

Syntax Completion: An editor that can suggest words (function names, variable names, etc) that have been used previously as you type saves an enormous amount of time and effort in tracking back to pieces of code for verification. More advanced editors may even convert partial code to completed blocks from built-in or plug-in templates.

Project Visualization: Any text editor will open a file, but being able to see an entire directory or folder structure and the files contained in them is invaluable and will keep you from having to switch back and forth between a file explorer or finder window over and over.

building greatness 4

Now you have access to tools whereby you can scaffold a basic application and begin developing, but you may not be prepared for success. Even seasoned developers can get caught up in the excitement of developing for a new platform and forget to plan ahead for the success they want and expect.

The next few pages should serve as advice to embarking on a development project using the PhoneGap platform with little to no experience in developing for it. If, however, you consider yourself a more seasoned developer, you may wish to jump forward a bit into some of the case studies in the Plug-In Wonderland chapter.

Even if you are looking to experiment a bit and test out the capabilities of the PhoneGap system, I highly encourage you to define some parameters for your project. What do you want the app to do? Who will be using it, even in a fictitious sense? If you were to begin writing PhoneGap hybrid mobile applications for others, they would (and do) expect to give you some guidelines on how it will function and, most likely, the style of the app.

As you begin to narrow down the scope of your project and understand what you need to accomplish—and, just as importantly, what you do not need to accomplish—you reduce the possible headaches you encounter in development. The example in table 4.1 is meant as an introductory guide for holding that pre-development Q&A necessary to define the direction you are heading and is not meant to be a guide for managing client-based production work.

4.1: Pre-Development Q&A	
Question	**Answer**
What is the app called?	*My Favorite Locations*
Who will use it?	*Anyone, but probably people over the age of 10.*
Why will they use it?	*To see some of my favorite spots and possibly visit them themselves.*
What are the key features of the app?	*Map overview with pins showing locations I tag, popups describing why they are my favorites, and a button to indicate they agree with the choice.*
What technologies are required to implement the features above?	*GPS, a database somewhere, probably some user tracking*

As you can see, there is a lot of functionality even in this example application and even more details to work out: what icon to use, what color scheme, what platforms to target, and so on. But this gives us a place to start and, I believe, successfully demonstrates the need for some planning up front.

After this small exercise, your head might start swimming with ideas for where you could take the app. For the example, it isn't a stretch to think that I want an administrative side of the app, so I could quickly add new places: snap a picture, geolocate to the place where I am at, add some data to a few fields, and save it to the database. Before you know it, the scope of this simple application begins to grow larger and larger. At some point, you could look at the chunk of development needed and wonder how you will ever get it developed and out the door for your audience to consume.

This is where the idea of minimum viable product, or MVP, is critical. MVP is the concept of approaching product development with an eye on iteration whereby you decide what the most critical and necessitated functions or features are for the product to be useful. For app development purposes, this can help you define the sometimes blurry line between a timely, cost-effective release that caters to the desired audience and a money-burning sinkhole of time that over delivers and might overwhelm users with complexity.

In the prior example, the audience likely will not care if an administrative portion is available since they are only consuming the output and not adding favorites of their own. If I can speed through development a bit faster and keep the scope of development more lean through my first version, I have less moving parts (opportunities for failure), less time required to produce the app (time is money), and can gauge the overall interest in the app before coming back to the table to plan a new version.

However, make sure you don't lose those great ideas for the next version. Create a document that serves as a "parking lot" for all of the ideas, not only concerning the development of the app, but also elements that may come to mind for marketing, sales, and other such activities. Too often have I gotten to the end of a product development cycle and been asked, "What is the next big feature?" and not remembered to stow ideas away for the occasion.

Larger projects that are coordinated across a larger team may wish to utilize a development roadmap—a way of taking the "parking lot" items and current development goals and layering them onto a calendar. This allows the development team (and, possibly, the public) to know what features are coming and when they can expect them. It also allows product managers and other influencers to weigh in on priorities and get visibility for your hard work.

Next, I find it helpful to understand the experience you expect the user to have in engaging with your PhoneGap hybrid mobile app. Defining what the user will see, hear, and do when interacting with the app can help you in developing key features in such a way so as not to miss important, desirable interactions and even avoid unnecessary functions.

One method for doing this is to write user stories. In capturing the "who," "what," and "why" of an interaction, you are also recording the "playback" for a well-written app. If you have never written user stories before, keep it simple: write sentences that describe who is doing what and what the result is. An example of a user story is below and is a longer version than typical. Often they are single sentences that dictate a small aspect of the intended functionality.

4.2: User Story Example
As a user of the *My Favorite Locations* app, I can login to the app using my email address and a password. Once logged in, I can scroll through a list of places that the author has added and pick any of them. When I pick one, I can see a picture of the place and some information about it including an address. If I click on the address, it will load the map on my phone so I can get directions to go there.

Drawing from the user story above and in mixing in the influence of other plans you have drawn, you should have enough information to begin forming an architectural outline of the app you wish to build as well as the support systems you may utilize: databases, web services, etc.

Creating the architectural documentation is one of the last steps in the "pre-game" regimen for my development practice. It consists of clearly documented steps for the app to engage in a web service, the format of data expected to be sent as well as returned, defining any security considerations and the requirements for those interactions, as well as managing resources on the device. The goal of the architecture document is to create a clear blueprint for what needs to be developed and often serves as a checkpoint in client communication to prevent misunderstandings in expectations.

To gain a better understanding of the structure and content of an architecture definition, an example has been provided (see figure 4.3: Architecture Definition Example). While there are more sections you can add and certainly some you may remove, this type of document can enable great communication with both technical and non-technical individuals on your team. In the event that you are a solo developer, it helps maintain a sense of what needs to be done and can assist in defining bite-sized segments and features to work on.

4.3: Architecture Definition Example
Overview *[Here you provide a high-level description of what the app will do, who will use it, and why they will use it.]* **Walkthrough** • *[Here you insert bulleted items representing the steps of operation from the moment the user taps the app icon. Branching logic should be represented here as well with clear paths to events and important input and output from the app. As you might imagine, this will most likely make up a huge portion of the document.]* • Display splash screen while app loads • Check internet connection and sync updated characters and player data if available • Ask user to choose a character and show all available characters as images • Load character data from local storage… **Databases** • Client-side   o *[This is where you define the tables and fields that will be used by the application. Since nearly every app has need of local data storage,*

be sure to put some thought into this structure.]

- Table: *Settings*
  - id – *Auto-incrementing long integer, primary key*
  - key – *Key for saving/retrieving the setting*
  - value – *Value; could be anything*

- Server-side
  - *[Here you may define server-side database tables and fields that will be utilized. This becomes important in the likely event that you will access web services for moving data back and forth.]*
  - Table: *Users*
    - id – *Auto-incrementing long integer, primary key*
    - name – *Name of user*
    - active – *Determines if user can log in*

Web Services

- *[Here you can provide a breakdown of web services your app will connect to.]*
- Host: *api.clickincrazy.com*
  - /login – *Submits credentials and receives the associated user token and latest statistics in return*
    - Out Parameters:
      - id (optional): *Can be used in lieu of username and password if id is already known (stored locally). If omitted, must pass username/password combination.*
      - username (optional): *If id is omitted, required string; also the email address of the user when they registered.*

- password (optional): *If id is omitted, required string; must be encoded using the app secret key before transmission.*

- Result:
  - id: *Unique id of the associated user.*
  - score: *Current score of the user.*

Version Control

[Here you describe the controls you wish to utilize in managing source control. This may be instructions on how or when to use new branches or tags.]

Branches will be defined by the sprint number and order as dictated by the PMO. Tagging is to be utilized for all major features as defined in the KEY FEATURES section…

With this document completed and a clear sight to the end product, we can dig into the actual code and see how to enable native functionality. In order to do that, we will need to access some PhoneGap plug-ins.

5 plug-in wonderland

PhoneGap utilizes a standardized plug-in interface for all access to native features including GPS, accelerometers, cameras, and file storage. These plug-ins can work in concert to produce apps that look and feel like a native counterpart.

The plug-in interface can also provide access to peripherals and APIs outside of the phone or mobile device itself. For instance, several companies and individuals have provided plug-ins for using Bluetooth LE to access a user's proximity to a Bluetooth beacon—or iBeacon, as it is sometimes called.

Many of the plug-ins you will include in your projects when getting started will come from the Apache Cordova team. Many were, before even version 3 of PhoneGap, included in the PhoneGap distribution by default. In the interest of creating a smaller footprint and following their own plug-in framework ("eating their own dog food," as it is sometimes called), the team moved them out to their own modules.

The first step is to consider the type of functionality required and find the corresponding plug-in, if it is available. For example, I may wish to add an in-game notification at the end of each level in our Clickin' Crazy game that would display how much time it took the player to finish the level and a congratulatory message. With the "what" in mind, I would open a web browser and head over to the Apache Cordova Plug-in Registry found at:

http://plugins.cordova.io

From the Repository web site, developers can browse or search all Cordova (and, thus, PhoneGap) plug-ins. For this example, we might search the word "notification" and find several entries for various types of notifications.

Another great resource for finding common plug-ins is the online PhoneGap documentation for developers found at:

http://docs.phonegap.com

From the PhoneGap documentation web site, I will find a link to the Plug-in APIs. This section of the documentation lists several of the plug-ins that are available. A quick perusal of the list would bring me across a mention of a "visual device notifications" plug-in. By following the link, I am redirected to a GitHub repository for the plug-in. If you are unfamiliar with GitHub, have a look at inset *5.1: A Word About GitHub.*

5.1: A Word About GitHub
If you are unfamiliar with GitHub, the site serves as a visual interface to a multitude of open source projects that utilize it as a repository for their code. Many plug-ins for PhoneGap are hosted on GitHub amongst many other project types and, as such, you will almost always find yourself back at GitHub when looking for a good plug-in to implement.

Reading through the documentation in the GitHub repository for the "Dialog" plug-in gives information on how to go about installing it and how to begin using it. The first step is to retrieve a copy of the code that makes it work and inject that code into our fledgling mobile app. The instructions indicate I should run the following:

```
cordova plugin add org.apache.cordova.dialogs
```

You might note that the command begins with a call to Cordova, the underlying toolchain PhoneGap is based on. This may feel a little foreign already given we have been using commands that begin with phonegap to interact with our specific app instance. That feeling turns out to be appropriate.

PhoneGap has integrated or aliased (depending on the case) each call to the Cordova framework so that developers can typically just replace the word "cordova" in a given example with "phonegap" and yield the same—or at the least desired—result. So, when I read the aforementioned command, I translate it as such:

```
phonegap plugin add org.apache.cordova.dialogs
```

If I execute the command from within the command prompt and context of the mobile app, the toolset will read the namespace we are adding ("org.apache.cordova.dialogs") and attempt to locate it in the default plug-in repository on GitHub. Once located, the plug-in is cloned into the mobile app folder and placed inside a "plugins" folder.

5.2: Alternatives to Namespaces

Installing a plug-in for PhoneGap works just as written for all core plug-ins published into the Apache GitHub account for this purpose, but a small change is required if you are installing a plug-in from a 3rd party. In this case, the PhoneGap system may not be able to translate the namespace back to an actual URL for retrieving and cloning the code. Instead, you can replace the namespace with the git repository's URL. Further, this means you should not feel confined to locating plug-ins on GitHub as any viable git repository (though, as mentioned before, GitHub does serve as the current standard for such things).

Now that the code is in place, I can look to further integrate the plug-in inside the app code for Clickin' Crazy. According to the documentation, the addition of this particular plug-in causes the following new methods to become available to the application:

navigator.notification.alert() – Show a custom dialog box
navigator.notification.confirm() – Show a custom confirmation box
navigator.notification.prompt() – Show a custom dialog with text entry
navigator.notification.beep() – Play a beep sound

Much more detail is available in the documentation, but I have distilled it to the essentials for our purposes. A quick look through the descriptions leads me to believe the "alert" method might be the best option for quickly noting the score (and other statistics) to the user without expecting a lot of interaction with the dialog box itself.

I would then dive into my Clickin' Crazy code and look for the point in which I want to show the dialog box with the score and execute the appropriate method:

```
navigator.notification.alert(
  "Your current score is: " + playerScore,
  function() {//do something if they click ok},
  "Clickin' Crazy Score",
  "Got it!");
```

For the example, I have added unnecessary line breaks to delineate the individual parameters that are passed to the function. In it, I indicate the *message* I want sent (the score), an empty *callback function* that I may use in the future, a *title* for the dialog box, and a *button name* I want displayed for the user to dismiss the dialog box.

At this point, many people might pop open the app and take a look at it in Chrome or one of the other browsers often used to debug PhoneGap hybrid mobile apps, as mentioned previously. Those people might be surprised or disheartened by what they find: the popup doesn't occur at all or, if it does, it looks like a generic browser-based alert with none of the custom formatting or style expected.

The reason for this behavior is that the plug-ins are officially injected into the mobile app at build time, not at design time. This means you might not see the fruits of your plug-in additions until you run a build and look at the resulting binary on a supported device. However, you can preview your app using the PhoneGap Developer app (installed on a compatible device) and gain access to core plug-ins—the plug-ins that are maintained in the Apache GitHub repository.

The PhoneGap Developer app is covered in more detail in the Debugging chapter ahead, but inset *5.3: The PhoneGap Developer App* serves as a jumpstart to using the tool.

5.3: The PhoneGap Developer App
To begin using the PhoneGap Developer app, first find and install the corresponding app published in your devices app store. A quick search for "phonegap" should narrow the results down and make it easier to locate. Once installed, return to your development machine and ensure that you are connected via wi-fi or otherwise to a network that is also accessible to a mobile device. Often this means ensuring that your phone or tablet is on the same wi-fi network as your development machine. This is crucial as the device and development machine must be able to directly communicate with each other. Once you establish mutual connectivity, you may run the PhoneGap host. To do so, open a command prompt and navigate to your PhoneGap app

project folder. From within the root of the folder, run the following command:

```
phonegap serve
```

The command should result in some output to the screen including an IP address and port in the format of:

```
[phonegap] listening on 192.168.1.100:3000
```

At this point you are ready to launch the PhoneGap Developer app on your mobile device. Once loaded, it will ask you to enter the information provided by the host. Simply type in the IP address (represented by "192.168.1.100" above) as well as the port (":3000") into the URL space of the app and press the button to connect.

Barring network connectivity issues, you should be viewing your app as it was designed to look on your mobile device with all the interactivity intended.

From testing the Clickin' Crazy app, I would be able to see the dialog boxes popup and confirm I have both the plug-in installed correctly and the code properly formed to instantiate it.

The dialog is just a small example of the great things plug-ins can do for you and your mobile app. Other great plug-ins exist that can perform amazing feats for you without engaging in the native layer. You can find these both by searching GitHub or by using the Cordova Plug-in Registry located on the web at http://plugins.cordova.io.

If you happen to find yourself in a situation where you need to engage with the native OS, since you cannot find a plug-in that fits your needs, there are two things to consider. First, you should consider taking a plug-in that is available publicly and modifying it to your needs. Often I find the gap between "exactly what I want" and "useless" is relatively small and something that can be patched or added to. Many of the plug-in authors put their works on GitHub for exactly this reason.

The second consideration is this: creating or modifying a plug-in is not very difficult, though it is an advanced topic. As such, you can find more about this in the What Lies Beyond chapter later in this book.

5.4: Other Great Plug-ins
I include this brief table containing some of my favorite plug-ins that are not a part of the core Apache Cordova plug-in series in the hopes you can more clearly see the possibilities plug-ins open for you. **BarcodeScanner** (https://github.com/wildabeast/BarcodeScanner) As its name implies, this plug-in gives native barcode recognition to your app. This opens up the ability to process the currently-popular QR Code variety of barcode as well as classic UPC formats and many others in-between. **EmailComposer** (https://github.com/katzer/cordova-plugin-email-composer) If you are writing business apps, it is highly likely you will need to send email. This plug-in makes that process incredibly easy while also keeping the user within your app—an important experiential element.

a better UI 6

One of the principal challenges I have encountered in developing hybrid mobile experiences comes back to user interface (UI) development. PhoneGap provides no default UI framework to begin with and this leads most PhoneGap developers to turn to a 3rd party UI framework. Additionally, a developer of such apps must have an appreciation for the various UI elements that have become standard on the different mobile operating systems.

For instance, iOS currently utilizes a flat user interface system where buttons are turned into simple 2-color text elements or simple icons. Android, on the other hand, has turned to a new UI design pattern—called "material"—that maintains button outlines. This description is incredibly simplistic, but is meant to demonstrate one simple design difference on two popular mobile operating systems.

Thankfully there are UI frameworks available that specifically cater to developing cross-platform hybrid mobile apps and strive to provide a native look despite, the nature of such projects. Some current examples include Kendo UI from Telerik (http://www.telerik.com/kendo-ui) and ChocolateChip-UI from Sourcebits (http://chocolatechip-ui.com/).

While the two aforementioned frameworks are meant to provide the look and feel of native UI design, you might also decide that this isn't an important design consideration for you. Further, you may actively decide to make the apps operate and appear identically on various devices; there are certainly times when having a consistent user experience is valuable. I often imagine a user on Android being able to pick up the iOS version and instantly knowing how to use the app due to this consistency. That decision, however, should be made on a per-project basis and may evolve over time.

If you decide to work with a consistent user experience across all platforms or want to manage the various user experience designs yourself, you may wish to turn to some of the other popular UI frameworks available. jQuery Mobile (http://jquerymobile.com/), an extension of the jQuery library, serves to provide a themeable, platform agnostic approach to the UI design.

Now you have an awareness of a few possibilities, it is time to see what these look like in practice. Since jQuery Mobile tends to be the first UI framework utilized by hybrid mobile app developers who are starting out, we will utilize it for our examples. It is important to remember, however, that each framework has its own syntax, styled outputs, and limitations. It is important to understand each of these before committing to one over another for a given project.

I will use the Clickin' Crazy app concept for demonstrating some of the widgets in jQuery Mobile. Specifically, we will look at one of the critical components of the app: the action-oriented button that must be repeatedly clicked to reach the next level. Before we can do any of that, we need the core framework downloaded and included in our hybrid mobile app.

jQuery Mobile runs on the jQuery JavaScript library. If you are not currently using the jQuery library in your app you will need to download it first. jQuery can be found at http://jQuery.com. Make sure you download the latest stable version and, once downloaded, copy the minified version of the library to your hybrid mobile app project's "js" folder (found within the "www" folder). The minified version is distinguishable from the others by containing the ".min" moniker in the file name.

You will also need to ensure a script reference is included in your "index.html" file also found in the "www" folder. The line needed to include the file will vary due to the ever-incrementing nature of the library's version number. However, the basics of it are the same as it would be for a normal HTML web site with the x, y, and z placeholders being replaced by the appropriate version numbers used in the file name.

```
<script type="text/javascript" src="js/jquery-x.y.z.min.js"></script>
```

To get jQuery Mobile in your project, download the current release from the web site. You can find it by navigating your web browser to:

http://jquerymobile.com/

Once on the site, look for large indicators to download jQuery Mobile. You may have the option between the "latest stable" version or a "custom download" package. I recommend using the former until you are more comfortable exploring the various options available in both this and other framework releases.

Just as you would have with the base jQuery library, copy the minified (with ".min" in the file name) to the "js" folder of your project and then add the reference to the specific version you copied using a tag such as :

```
<script type="text/javascript" src="js/jquery.mobile-x.y.z.min.js">
</script>
```

In addition to copying the minified JavaScript library file you will also have need to copy the base CSS file and images to your "css" project folder. The CSS file will follow the format of "jquery.mobile-x.y.z.min.css" where the version number replaces the "x.y.z" letter notation. The entire "images" subfolder of your jQuery Mobile download should be copied into the "css" folder of your hybrid mobile app project. This might seem strange, but the pre-determined pathways to the images used by the jQuery Mobile framework are relative to the location of the CSS file. While this can be altered, this is the easiest way to get started.

Once copied, you will also need to reference the style sheet you just copied. This can be achieved by adding the following line while also modifying for the version number as you have for other such elements:

```
<link rel="stylesheet" type="text/css" href="css/jquery.mobile-x.y.z.min.css" />
```

Finally, you are ready to take advantage of the widgets and automatic styling that such a framework can provide. As I said before, we are going to focus on the action button. In my vision of this, we have a bright red button that spans the width of the screen and says “Power Up!”

Because jQuery Mobile will automatically style *button* elements for you, I would choose to use specific tag:

```
<button class=”actionButton”>Power Up!</button>
```

This is all it takes to create the button, but it lacks the red background that would really drive attention to it and encourage the user to mash away on it. To accomplish this, I can simply change the *background-color* attribute in my “index.css” file. It is also crucial that we add the *!important* modifier to the end of our style entry in the CSS file in order to override the default styling jQuery Mobile provides.

Whatever UI framework you choose, be sure to thoroughly peruse the documentation to understand any nuances to implementing the framework. Often there are best practices published that can aid in more quickly or efficiently producing the desired affect.

Along with the consideration for which UI framework to use (if any), there should be a consideration for what graphics will be used within the application. Further, you should be prepared to create or modify your images or graphics to maintain a higher resolution so as to maintain their fidelity when scaling to larger devices and/or devices with higher pixel density. This also has play when styling your CSS: designing something to span the entire width of the screen may work fine for a phone in portrait mode, but can have unintended visual consequences when viewed on a tablet or even landscape orientation on a phone.

One popular method for preparing for the nuances of hybrid mobile design is to create a style guide for the app. Style guides may contain everything from font selections, color palettes, logo positioning, button styling, and more. In the particular case that you are working for or with others, the style guide can provide a visual communications mechanism for sorting through potential design hazards early on, well before code begins to be written.

Lastly—and I cannot stress this point enough—a good design must embrace the different device formats. Views and layouts that are created with a phone's portrait orientation in mind often do not translate well to a landscape-oriented tablet device. The expectations of usability are different, so be prepared to design different user interfaces accordingly.

7 debugging

Debugging is a crucial component of any development effort and is just as critical in hybrid mobile app development. PhoneGap provides very few mechanisms directly for debugging, but the proliferation of developer tools in modern browsers has led to some powerful debugging mechanisms being available right under our noses.

One of the easiest, cross-platform debugging tools available is the developer console in Google's Chrome web browser. Using it is simple and fast. If you do not have an updated or current copy of Google's Chrome browser (hereafter referred to simply as "Chrome") installed, you can install it on your development machine by visiting the following URL in a web browser and following the downloading and installing instructions:

http://www.google.com/chrome/

Once Chrome is installed, you can get to your project by typing the path to your project's "www/index.html" file into the navigation bar of an open Chrome window. As it loads (or after it loads), you can access the developer console using one of the following methods, depending on your machine's operating system:

Windows: Control - Shift - J keyboard shortcut
or View > Developer > JavaScript Console in the menu

Linux: Control - Shift - J keyboard shortcut
or View > Developer > JavaScript Console in the menu

Mac: Command - Option - J keyboard shortcut
or View > Developer > JavaScript Console in the menu

With the Chrome developer console open, we have access to some top-notch debugging utilities. The first is the JavaScript console—an area that PhoneGap developers seem to consistently spend most of their time in while debugging. The reason this area is so important is simple: the text output found here serves as a sort of "canary in the mineshaft" for JavaScript development and alerts developers to the smallest script failures as well as errors in loading network resources.

Items such as those described above show up as red text (by default) against the gray or white background—a quick cue to the developer's eye that something is amiss. In addition to the error logging capabilities, the Chrome JavaScript console enabled you to execute arbitrary JavaScript code within the context of the current window. That means you are able to examine the values of global variables (window-scoped variables) and even execute public functions or object methods if accessible.

In applying this to the demonstration app of Clickin' Crazy, let's assume I have a function on my action page that executes on the tap event of an image:

```
function didClickCrazily() {
  console.log(currentScore);
}
```

In this example, I am using console.log, the common logging object and method found in modern browsers, to send output to the Chrome JavaScript console. In the event I am concerned that the function isn't firing (because I don't see any "currentScore" data populating in the console when I perform the tap that should execute this code), I have a few remedies available.

First, I might try to execute the function directly in the console by typing a call to it just as I would in JavaScript found in my pages:

```
didClickCrazily()
```

I should either be presented with the expected result (a currentScore value) or I might be presented with something unexpected, such as a null value. The latter would indicate that I have improperly scoped my JavaScript variable or not initialized it to the expected value elsewhere. Regardless, I now have a clue as to where the problem may be and can continue to debug (via the console or otherwise) to locate the offending issue.

Another element of the debugging console worth noting is the network activity tab. As your projects become more complex, you will likely find yourself making calls to web services. Depending on various factors, some of which are out of your control, those calls to external resources may fail or return unexpected results. Once again the console comes to the rescue by allowing you to trace back the request (including data payloads) as well as the response back from the remote server.

Often the findings from such debugging sessions are a combination of frustrating and relieving; I may be expecting to receive an array of objects when I am actually receiving an associative array (object hash of objects) that breaks the method I am using for iterating through the results. I am thankful, however, that I can trace back the response and see what data types are being returned upstream to quickly eliminate potential failure points and allow me to focus on the real issue at hand.

Another great feature of the developer console that I must mention is the ability to emulate various device screen sizes and behaviors (including user-agent headers). Activating this feature can be done by clicking the "mobile phone" icon in the toolbar of the developer console. Once activated, the view changes and allows the selection of a device to emulate. Available devices range from Apple iPhone models, Samsung Galaxy devices, and more. By changing devices and orientations, you can easily test your media queries or overall responsiveness of your app in different environments.

I would be remiss if I didn't caution you on one point here: while emulation is highly valuable and goes a long way towards reducing the frustrations of a deployed device not "behaving" as intended, emulation is not a replacement for actual device testing and debugging. Too many times have I relied upon massive emulation efforts to validate the use cases and styling in CSS only to have someone in the quality assurance (QA) stages hold a phone or tablet up to me that looked significantly different than what I would have expected to see.

My last suggestion for debugging is the PhoneGap Developer app. This app, available in your device's app store, allows you to test your mobile app in a native environment with conditions that are the nearest to "deployed" conditions without actually committing to a build and deployment cycle. The basic setup and usage is covered in inset *5.3: The PhoneGap Developer App* found in the Plug-In Wonderland chapter. Here, however, I would like to discuss some of the caveats of aforementioned debugging methods as well as usage of the PhoneGap Developer app.

One substantial limitation to the JavaScript console debugging, while loading files on your local machine, is the inherent security limitation on data access. If you find yourself with a need to synchronize files or otherwise store files on your client devices as a feature or function of your mobile app, you will quickly discover that permanent and temporary storage access is intentionally limited by browser security features.

The limitations present themselves in various ways depending on the browser and operating system you are using, but requests to initialize storage will be rejected and, often, a generic error message given. There are browser "hacks" that can enable a developer to get around these important precautions implemented by the browsers, but I believe a more material approach to this issue is in how you access the app to begin with.

Accessing the app in a built and deployed environment (running on the device as an intended end-product) will not make it subject to the same security restrictions. This is important as developers are often inclined to over-engineer a solution to the debugging problem before they realize the relatively limited scope of the issue.

Aside from building and deploying the app to test the real behavior of the storage mechanism, there is an even easier solution: host your project on a web server. By accessing your project from a non-local URL, the browser enables storage solutions and will stop flatly denying storage initialization requests. While this may not necessarily be the blocking issue, checking this will prevent you from re-engineering solutions over and over again fruitlessly.

Another limitation you might encounter is that the PhoneGap Developer app does not import specific plug-ins from your project, only a standard set that ships with the PhoneGap Developer app. That means that any custom plug-ins will not be supported and can induce errors in testing the app via this method.

The only real protection from this behavior is a solid development practice: check for the presence of plug-in markers in the window or navigation objects before attempting to access those plug-in objects. This makes your project more stable and has the additional benefit of easing the transition from a built and deployed app to a web-hosted companion version.

You will find that the landscape of debugging will continue to shift even as you enter into PhoneGap development, but these tools have continued to evolve with time and have improved the debugging experience.

prepping for release

8

In this chapter I will give you some pointers on items that need to be resolved for a successful build and deployment cycle. The crucial components to such a build are fairly simple: code that runs without bugs in debugging, appropriate image assets, app store credentials (if deploying to the app store), and a device or simulator for testing.

If you have a project that continues to be troublesome in debugging before making it to the build phase, I advise you to stop now and go back to debugging. Bugs in your software will only be exacerbated by the build and deployment process and make debugging significantly more difficult from within the native wrapper. The only exception to this might be, as noted earlier in this book, the case of certain storage conventions and native hardware components that cannot be appropriately simulated or emulated outside of a semi-deployed environment.

The next piece that must be locked is the assembly of image assets—icons and splash screens. The devices and configurations you may wish to deploy to directly influence the quantity and configuration of the various images that should be created. By default, for instance, PhoneGap ships with a series of icons and splash screens that feature the same "build robot." One nice thing about these seemingly-useless default icons: they serve as a guide for the dimensions and pixel density for the icons and splash screens you ultimately need to create for inclusion with your app build(s).

To find these icons and splash screens, you need only look in the "www" folder of a PhoneGap project for a "res" subfolder. Within this "res" subfolder will exist both an "icon" and "screen" folder with a subfolder for each mobile OS supported by the PhoneGap build process. By examining the contents of a given "icon" or "screen" subfolder, developers can examine the constituent files needed to target that device OS.

Splash screen images found in the subfolders of the "screen" folder can seem a bit complex, but are created to fit a combination of device sizes, display densities, and device orientations (landscape vs. portrait). Each image is static and created to span the entirety of the display on the device it is meant to target and the name of the file is what actually links back to the specific device configuration it is intended for.

Icon images found in the "icon" subfolders are quite similar to the splash screen images in that they are created to cater to different devices and display densities (though without the concern for device orientation). Icons, however, may contain versions targeting different functions on different devices such as a settings icon, a taskbar icon, and a launch icon. As with the splash screens, the naming convention of the image files inform the PhoneGap build system as to which device configuration they are intended for. It is possible to modify the names of these files, but it is not recommended for introductory development.

When replacing the images for either splash screens or icons, be sure to use the same dimensions and aspect ratio as the file you are replacing. For instance, if a file displays at 57 pixels by 57 pixels, the replacement image should maintain those exact dimensions. Failure to replace files with appropriately-sized files will lead to build failures later on or, in some cases, the icons simply showing as missing from the final product.

It is also important to understand you do not need to replace every file for every possible device OS. If you do not intend to deploy to the BlackBerry platform, for instance, there is no need to spend the extra time and effort to modify or replace those splash screen or icon files.

At this point you may be ready to begin performing builds and deploying to test devices or simulators. To build for a given platform you must inform PhoneGap of your intention to do so. This is done through the PhoneGap "platform" command which is structured similarly to the example below. Replace the "<platform>" placeholder with a valid device target. See inset *8.1: PhoneGap Device Platforms* for information on determining valid platform options.

```
phonegap platform add <platform>
```

With the platform added that you wish to target, you can attempt your first build with the following command (with "<platform>" placeholder replaced with the chosen device platform option):

phonegap build <platform>

When the build command is executed, the command terminal will jump into a frenzy, verbosely outputting each of the constituent commands that make up the PhoneGap build script for the chosen platform. While it is unlikely a developer watching the stream of text could make much sense of the output, it is wise to look for output that is colored red, as it is often an early indicator of a build that will fail. This isn't always the case, however, and may not apply to initial builds in particular.

8.1: PhoneGap Device Platforms
If you are unsure what device targets are available, you can always check by requesting a list from the PhoneGap toolkit using: phonegap platform list This command will produce a list of valid build targets that are compatible with the PhoneGap system and your current development environment. The list looks something like this: Available platforms: amazon-fireos, android, blackberry10, browser, ios, firefoxos

Once the stream of output ceases, you will receive either a "success" or "fail" message in the command output. In the event of a failure, look at the error specifics and find some guidance in the upcoming chapter on troubleshooting.

With a successful build, you are ready to test the build output on a real device or in a device simulator. The process for doing so varies significantly for each platform and will not be covered in detail here. I will, however, provide some basic guidance on getting the app onto a test device or in a simulator for the two most popular device OS targets (Android and iOS).

For all PhoneGap builds, the output is placed in the "platforms" subfolder of the main project root and then within a subfolder that is created for the specific platform the build was executed for. So, in the case of an Android build, you can find the resultant build in the "platforms/android" folder from within your project's root.

Android builds generate an APK file—an unsigned container used by the mobile operating system to install the app. An APK file is considered unsigned when it does not carry the credentials of the developer to indicate and validate the authenticity of the app. Installation on a device or submission to the Google Play Store, however, will require a signed version. Since certification and app store submission processes are outside the scope of this book, I will instead direct you to look through the Google Play Store's developer documentation for more information on these requirements and how best to adhere to them.

8.2: When the Project Name is the Default

If you are searching for your built application file and find that the naming convention is the default "HelloWorld" scheme, fear not. Simply open the "config.xml" file in the "www" folder of your project root and change the value found in the following tag to your desired name, save, and re-run the build process:

```
<name>HelloWorld</name>
```

While you are in there, you should check the "id" attribute of the "<widget>" XML tag as well and ensure it is set to an appropriate canonical ID as discussed in the *Generating Your App* chapter.

Once you have a *signed* APK, it can be placed on a web server so a test device can access the APK for installation via the corresponding URL. Installing an APK acquired from outside the Google Play Store, however, requires that the device explicitly set a configuration option on the device. This is commonly located in Settings → Security and is often labeled as "Unknown sources." Checking this option allows non-Play Store apps to be installed. It is important to note that this is a potential security risk, if left checked on a personal or professional device that does not exist solely for debugging.

The iOS build has many of the same requirements as Android and other mobile device operating systems in that an authenticated (or signed) version of the app is required to begin device testing. The process for signing an app with your developer certificate and installing on your device is well-documented by Apple and the latest versions of Xcode make this process easier than ever before. Unlike Android, however, there is no option to self-sign a binary distribution of the app and install on devices for debugging without having a valid Apple Developer account.

Lastly, I wish to provide some information on alternatives to the app store that you may not be aware of. While getting your app distributed via the app store for a given platform is an exciting mechanism for getting your work to the masses, there are times when an app's purpose or audience is so narrow that app store distribution simply doesn't make sense.

As an example, I have written a hybrid mobile app using PhoneGap that synchronizes the contact information for all employees in the company to the client device and authenticates the current user using an internal Active Directory system. Because the usage scope for this app is extremely narrow (only people within my company can or should have access), app store distribution simply didn't make sense.

In this case, I utilized an enterprise deployment model for app distribution. This often requires some additional credentials through the certifying entity (Apple, Google, Microsoft, etc), but allows the developer to bypass app store deployment and simply host a signed/certified mobile app on a web host for internal deployment. In my specific example, an internal web portal is used to distribute the app. There are limitations to what you can distribute and specifics around the intended audience, but it is important to acknowledge this alternative as a viable one.

troubleshooting

In development, sometimes things just don't go according to plan. New versions of software are released, new bugs are introduced, and whole new operating systems arrive to dazzle and, perhaps, frustrate.

There are a lot of things that can go wrong and in no way am I under the delusion that I can cover every case that might come up. So, my tactic is to provide you, the developer, with the array of go-to resources I turn to when something just isn't quite working well for me. The resources I have selected are well-maintained, have an active user community, and/or are responsible for saving my skin on more than one occasion. That being said, I can't resist taking a crack at a few of the more common issues that arise when getting started in hybrid mobile app development with PhoneGap.

First up, you might hit a roadblock early in the process of setting up your environment for development and find that none of the example

PhoneGap commands ("phonegap") will run for you. The most common reason for this is missing the crucial "-g" parameter when installing PhoneGap to begin with. As a reminder, Node.js reads this parameter as a signal to install the PhoneGap framework "globally" (hence the "g" in "-g"), allowing the framework commands to be ran from any path and not just the specific path the PhoneGap toolset is installed to. This issue is easily remedied by re-installing PhoneGap using the correct parameter:

npm install –g phonegap

Next is the trouble with upgrading. As I mentioned before, new versions of mobile and desktop operating systems are released all the time. When this happens, new feature are added and, often, old features are discontinued. When this happens, you may find that an update to your existing app is necessary. While there is no single "silver bullet" to cure this woe, I recommend keeping an eye on the release notes for any major PhoneGap release via the web site at http://phonegap.com. In particular, look for official blog posts detailing the bug fixes and known issues for a given release.

Lastly, you may run across an annoying delay in your application as you begin to test whereby click events seem to take an inordinate amount of time before responding. The funny thing about this particular bug is that the behavior is by design. The reason for this your browser forces a delay of approximately 300 milliseconds when a click event is initiated. The reason: it waits to see if you are going to click again in that time period, converting the "click" event into a "double-click" event.

While 300 milliseconds may not sound like very long, it can seem quite pronounced when you are trying to navigate a menu structure and want to get the same responsive feel as you get in native implementations. The great news is that there are multiple approaches to resolving this issue. Each has been outlined below in inset *9.1: Clicks and Taps.*

9.1: Clicks and Taps
One of the easiest ways to ensure the app bypasses the 300ms delay on click events is to not have click events. This may seem contrary to your goals, but it is not. While the easiest way to implement tap-enabled areas is to re-use the "click" event attached to anchor tags ("<a href='…'>") and the JavaScript onClick event, the HTML5 specification has explicit event trapping for tap events that are not subject to the 300ms delay. So, by converting anchors and onClick events to use the "tapstart" and "tapend" events you can avoid processing taps as clicks. This approach, admittedly, can be a chore and requires that you architect your code with a pattern that resembles the tap vs. click from the beginning or risk a lengthy re-engineering of existing code. Not the most appealing of choices and it certainly wasn't for me when the suggestion was given. Thankfully, there is a more global approach that caters to efficiency by reducing the amount of re-engineered code you may have while providing the end-user performance gains you want: the FastClick plugin. This small JavaScript library essentially transforms all standard click events into tap events seamlessly and, best of all, is free. You can download it on the web at https://github.com/ftlabs/fastclick.

Now that the list of the obvious issues are out of the way, let's dive into three valuable resources available to you on the web. Each one of these has been curated from a long line of sites and communities I belong to.

Stack Overflow (http://stackoverflow.com)

Part of the Stack Exchange network of sites generally dedicated to helping the user community in problem solving within a plethora of domains, the Stack Overflow site has become the de-facto standard first-stop for development troubleshooting assistance. The community is encouraged to answer questions and edit existing content (in a wiki-like fashion) through incentives such as badge, titles, and feature unlocking.

With over 1 million users, Stack Overflow is a forum were the burning question you have or the problem you are experiencing has probably already been discussed and finding it is quite easy. In the event you can't find what you are looking for, it is quite easy to ask a question on the site and get quality responses. From time to time you may be redirected to existing questions and answers, but these are almost always appropriate guides and, if nothing else, help you clarify your question or eliminate possible causes.

Additionally, the user community is self-policed; this adds a nice touch in that you can ask questions without much fear of a random individual bashing your request for help. When this does happen, such comments are swiftly removed ("moderated") and offending users appropriately notified.

PhoneGap Documentation (http://docs.phonegap.com/en)

The official documentation from the PhoneGap team offers a wide variety of resources that can be extremely useful in debugging or finding additional help. The platform guide sections help developers keep up with the latest nuances in developing for a given mobile operating system while the API reference sections maintain the latest core plug-ins you can use in your application without hunting through GitHub pages.

In addition, the latest features and fixes are documented in the pages within this site and can inform you of new opportunities to add polish to your app. Lastly, the ability to choose a specific, targeted version of the PhoneGap system enables the site documentation to "roll back" to a version you are working with to avoid the pitfalls of desynchronized documentation and implementation. That alone can dispel some of the ambiguity that can come from finding a wayward blog post on a topic that "should work" only to find that it doesn't.

Devgirl's Weblog (http://devgirl.org)

Holly Shinsky, a.k.a. Devgirl, has been blogging about web and mobile development for 6+ years and has become a strong voice in PhoneGap evangelism. That is probably why, as of this writing, she holds the title of Senior Technical Evangelist at Adobe Systems. The Devgirl Weblog has a long list of articles on various topics and many, especially in recent years, have revolved around PhoneGap.

Holly's insight into the ongoing maintenance and feature additions from within the Adobe camp make her blog a highly-valuable resource for keeping up with the latest tips and news in hybrid mobile development.

what lies beyond 10

As is the case with any introduction, we have only scratched the surface and there are a lot of areas you could explore from here. Once you master the basics of PhoneGap and settle on a UI framework (or multiple) that you are comfortable with, you will likely venture out and begin looking at the various plug-ins available for inspiration. Features you never thought to add to your app ideas are on-tap and at your fingertips.

One of the greatest parts of the PhoneGap architecture lies in the ability for any developer to become a plug-in developer. When I was introduced to iBeacons—Bluetooth Low-Energy (LE) devices that transmit some basic information at a fixed signal strength and polling period—I was fascinated with the possibilities. I almost immediately sketched the concept for a modern version of the "Hot and Cold" game I had played in my childhood where you walk around trying to find an object chosen by another person, and the only clues you are given are variations on getting "warmer" or "colder."

A potential roadblock was quickly encountered: there weren't any cross-platform PhoneGap plug-ins that supported the Bluetooth capabilities needed to poll for iBeacons and react as needed. I was able to find one for Android and another in-progress for iOS, but neither were bug-free and implementations were a bit rough. So, since I had not yet launched into plug-in development, I took the challenge as an opportunity to do just that. A few days later, I had way more of a Bluetooth LE than before and a plug-in with consistent interfaces for both Android and iOS that properly ranged for iBeacons.

If you are interested in new plug-in development or the further development and extension of an existing plug-in (remember, the source is out there to work with), definitely look at the resources the PhoneGap team has published on their developer portal on the web at http://docs.phonegap.com. There is a whole section dedicated to plug-in development and goes into quite a bit of detail on how to author your first one.

The PhoneGap team and the contributors to the Cordova framework are incredibly talented and creative. What started as a patch to pick up geolocation data has already been immensely transformative and I can't even guess at what the future holds for this innovative system. I look forward to seeing you on the hybrid mobile journey with me.

about the author

Matthew Ray (just "Matt," thank you) was born in Anderson, Indiana in 1979, the wisest, most attractive, and only son of Phil and Cathy Ray. He eventually was forced to share the house with a younger sister, Gina, eight years later. He later got revenge on this intrusion by methodically shaping his sister into a nerd, while simultaneously inflicting a multitude of games, Monty Python films, and episodes of the Tom Green Show upon her. Another eight years passed and he started a small (otherwise known as "solo") web development company in high school.

Matt was destined to attend an "Ivy League" college, so upon graduating high school, he immediately applied to and was accepted into Ivy Tech State College. He has since practiced the dark arts of web, client-server, and mobile development for several companies in Indiana.

He currently resides in Pendleton, Indiana with his soon-to-be wife (fingers crossed) Ashley and cuddles with his 9-year old daughter as often as possible.

@themattray http://blog.mattray.info

www.ingramcontent.com/pod-product-compliance
Lightning Source LLC
Chambersburg PA
CBHW071030050326
40689CB00014B/3588

* 9 7 8 1 5 0 0 1 8 7 7 0 5 *